Revolutiona

The true story of a teenager who was a spy for George Washington

By
Charles Courtsal

Illustrations by
Kitty Forbush

In answering y[our]
[I] begin with your great g[randfather]
[earl]y Wilson. He had thr[ee]
[sons and two] daughters – Uriah Jr., E[lizabeth?]
[Eliza]beth, Elnathan and Mar[y?]
[whe]n the Revolutionary Wa[r]
[Uria]h as captain and David
[one] day your grandfather [who]
[a]lso entered the army. Th[ey]
[the]y lay at White Plains,
[mile]s above New York. Eliza[beth]
[who lived near?] asian, acted as a spy for
I have written quite a det[ailed]
[th]e transaction as related
[near] sixty years ago. Eliz[abeth]

living yet. For aught I
David died at the [age]
of one hundred and six
told. Elnathan, my [father,]
[your] grand-father I c[an]
[re]collect. Before he came [to]
[o]f Wyoming he lived [in]
[in] Connecticut near N[ew]
[t]he Wilson family a[t]
[an]d a great part of the
which New London now
After the Revolution, [the]
[c]urrency began to depreci[ate]
[fi]nally became worthles[s]
[f]ather and his family [to]

OUR FAMILY TREE

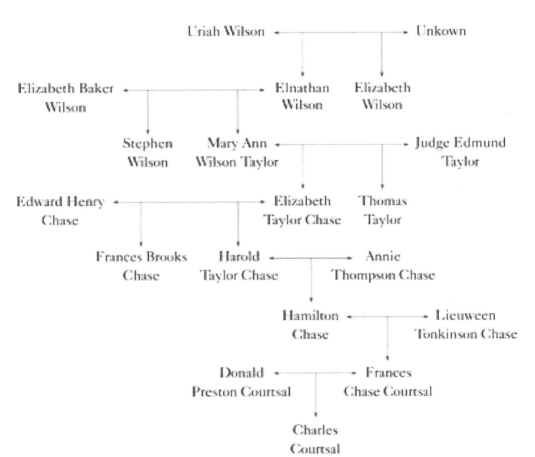

Uriah Wilson → ← → Unkown

Elizabeth Baker Wilson ← → Elnathan Wilson → Elizabeth Wilson

Stephen Wilson | Mary Ann Wilson Taylor ← → Judge Edmund Taylor

Edward Henry Chase ← → Elizabeth Taylor Chase | Thomas Taylor

Frances Brooks Chase | Harold Taylor Chase ← → Annie Thompson Chase

Hamilton Chase ← → Lieuween Tonkinson Chase

Donald Preston Courtsal ← → Frances Chase Courtsal

Charles Courtsal

One day during the winter of 1807, I was visiting my cousins in Pennsylvania during a terrible snowstorm. It was bitter cold, and the wind was howling. My uncle had a large home made of logs but their house moaned with the wind gusts. I was just 5 years old, and I was frightened. I was sure that the logs were going to blow away at any moment.

My aunt Elizabeth Wilson was finishing up her work in the kitchen and did not seem bothered by the storm at all. She was always calm and wise. To my eyes, she was very old, but probably all of 50 years old at the time.

When the house shook, she noticed that I was afraid, so she decided this was a good time to distract me and my cousins by telling us the story of her dangerous trip behind the British lines during the American Revolutionary War.

"Well children" she said, " come and sit by the fire. If you can listen quietly, I will tell you about my adventure as a spy."

It was 1776, the very beginning of the American Revolutionary War, and the British had captured all of New York City. General George Washington had retreated to White Plains, New York, with his troops.

General Thomas, an American General, was a prisoner in New York, but he had liberty to go anywhere in the city because he had given his parole (or word of honor) not to leave the city until permitted to do so by discharge or by prisoner exchange.

General Washington wanted to share some important information with him,
but this could not be done without great hazard to the life of anyone who should attempt it.

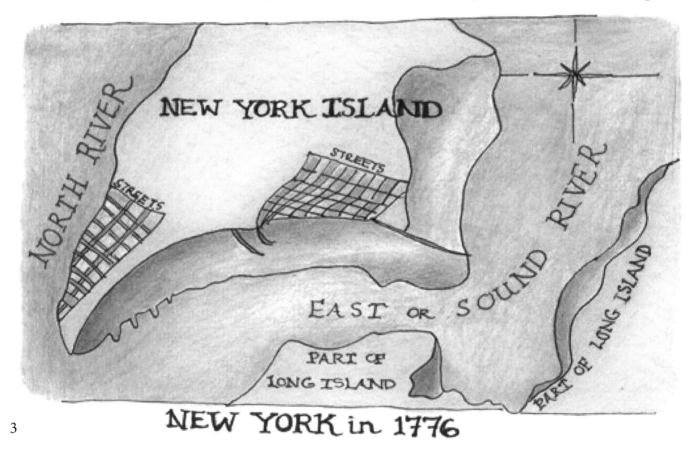

NEW YORK in 1776

At that time, our family lived not far from General Washington's headquarters.

One day, an American officer came to our home and asked to see me. My mother called for me and when I came to the door, the officer handed me a note. It was

a note from General George Washington, politely requesting me to call at his headquarters the next day at 10 o'clock am.

Can you imagine my surprise! I was only 19 years old!

After reading the note, I told the officer I would see the General the next day, as requested. He left, and I began to wonder what in the world General Washington wanted of me. My whole family was a little anxious and afraid of what might happen the next day. That night was a sleepless night for me.

So, I rose early in the morning and dressed myself in my best attire.

At precisely 10 o'clock, I knocked at the General's residence. A servant appeared at the door and I told him I wished to see General Washington. The General, who was nearby, heard my voice and immediately walked toward me, smiling. He extending his hand and said, "You are Miss Wilson, I presume?"

I replied, "Yes, I am the one to whom this note is addressed," and I showed him the note that was delivered to me the day before.

"Please walk in, Miss Wilson, and take a seat," he said, "I am glad to see you, although I almost regret getting you involved in this matter. There is a dangerous enterprise that I desire you to undertake."

He held in his hand a sheet of paper that was two-thirds filled with writing.

"I have a message of great importance that I would like to have delivered to General Thomas in New York City. "

"Miss Wilson, you have been most favorably recommended to me as an educated, intelligent young lady of caution, prudence, spirit and daring remarkable for your age and sex."

On this account, I wish to engage your service in conveying this message — but it is a hazardous and dangerous undertaking.

If you should be detected with the message in your possession, you would be hung or shot. The British have no mercy for rebels, as they call us, and especially rebel spies.

I replied; "General Washington, if you are willing to trust me with your message, I can convey your message to General Thomas without the possibility of discovery. I will commit it to memory and carry it in my mind where none but God can find it."

He said, "Yes, I am willing to entrust the secret to your safe keeping if you think you can commit it to memory and recite its contents for General Thomas, word for word as it is written here."

I replied, " If you give me the message and 30 minutes by myself, I will convince you of my ability to commit it to memory."

The General handed me the paper, opened a door into another room and said "You can slide into that room and be alone as long as you need to memorize the message." I went in, shut the door and commenced my task.

In less than half an hour, I came out and handed the paper to the General, who was writing at his desk, and recited its contents to him three or four times over. He seemed highly pleased and said, "Miss Wilson, you have every word in your head, but do you think you can remember the message clearly as you try to pass the British sentries and enter New York City by yourself? "

I answered, "General, if you meet me five years from now and I cannot repeat every word, you may hang me for a spy."

He laughed at my youthful confidence and said, " No, I won't do that. So, do you have a plan to make your way through the pickets of the British lines?"

"Yes", I said. "Country women with marketing of any kind are freely admitted into the city to sell or barter their goods for whatever they may want. I will dress myself as a farmer's daughter with a common calico or linsey wool dress.
I will wear my youngest brother's shoes, a coarse shawl over my shoulders and
a gingham sunbonnet on my head."

"I will take a market basket on my arm with a couple dozen eggs, two or three pounds of butter, a couple cakes of home-made soap and probably some other little trifles that I may think of. Then, I will have no fear of being prevented from going where I please in the city."

"However, General, if you had a small token that General Thomas would recognize as belonging to you, I could take it and show it to him. That way, he would know I am truly your messenger." The General remarked, "I see, Miss Wilson, that you are fully equal to this task and require no further instruction from me. When you return, please see me as soon as possible if you have a response from General Thomas. As for the token, I have here a little gold pencil given to me by a French officer, in the presence of General Thomas in the General's own home some time ago. Please take it, and I have no doubt the General will recognize it at once."

General Washington asked, "Do you need any money for your trip ?"
"No, General," I said, "I do not want any money from you now. If ever I take any, it will be when I take my harness off and not when I put it on." He smiled and said, "Very well, do as you please, Miss Wilson."
I then rose and said, "With your leave, I will now go home and get ready for my trip to New York City tomorrow."
He approached and took my hand. I looked up to him and repeated the message while he held my hand. He said, "Every word right. God bless you and God bring your enterprise to a successful conclusion." Then, he bid me "Good Bye."

Early the next morning, I was on my way to the city and before noon, I approached the outer pickets of the British army. I stopped and asked the sentinels permission to go into the city with my marketing.

The guard stepped up to me, asked where I lived and what I had to sell. I showed him the contents of my basket, and he said I could pass on.

But before I got too far into the city, another Redcoat guard stopped me and asked me several questions, all of which I answered to his satisfaction, I suppose, for he told me I could go on and that I would have no further delays.

Moments later I overheard another soldier talking. He had been standing next to the second guard who had stopped me. He said to the guard, "She seems awfully well educated and well spoken for a market woman. Had you not better call her back and question her, examine her more closely?"

"No, I think not," said the guard. "She is some farmer's wench that feels proud of being in New York City and carries a high head."

Even though I felt offended by these final comments, I made sure to hurry along into the city. I soon found the street in which General Thomas lived. Then, I found his home and went to the door and knocked.

Presently the door was opened by a servant girl. I asked if General Thomas lived here. She said, "Yes."

"Is he at home?, I asked and she said, "No."

"Is Mrs. Thomas?"

"Yes, but she don't want any marketing."

"I have nothing to sell her, but I must see her."

When she heard this, she tried to slam the door in my face, which I prevented by placing my foot against the door. She then went in, and I heard her say, "There is an impudent country woman at the door who says she will not go away without seeing you."

"Well," said Mrs. Thomas, "I'll go and see what she wants."

With a stern look she came to where I was standing, but the moment I said.

"Madam, I have a message for General Thomas," her face relaxed its sternness and she said, "You can hand it to me."

"No, Madam, I can give the message to no one but the General himself."

A few moments later, the General and his wife came in and I told him I had a message from General Washington. He stared at me and looked rather incredulous.

I said, "General Thomas, I have a token from General Washington to prove my honesty", and I showed him the little gold pencil.

I continued, " General Thomas, you know it would be death to me to be detected as a spy. So, I have memorized a message from General Washington for you. Please take paper and pen and write down my words as I repeat them to you. Then, you will have the message."

Although he looked a little dubious, he got paper and pen and commenced to write as I dictated my message. When he was through, he looked the message over once or twice and seemed very surprised and even delighted with its contents.

Then, he wished to know my name, residence, etc. and how I got through the guards with my disguise. I told him why I was dressed as he saw me and what I had in my market basket.

The General asked Mrs. Thomas to take the contents of my market basket and pay me market prices for them, as they had use for them all. Then, he said, I should buy some items in town to show the sentinels when I leave the city.

Due to the late hour, I could not leave until the next day, so the General asked that I remain his guest until I was ready to go.

He guessed that I was probably hungry and said that tea would soon be ready. He asked me to make myself perfectly at home.

I began to make some apologies about my clothing when he kindly said, "Now Miss Wilson, none of that. We know perfectly why you are wearing this calico dress and coarse shawl. It is exactly as it should be for the occasion, and we welcome you as if you were attired in the richest of silks."

Then, he said he would like to send a return message to General Washington if I would take the trouble to hide it in the same secure place. I asked him to write it down and I would try to memorize it. He agreed and wrote down the message until we were told the tea was ready. While at the table, he said, " I am afraid you will find it a hard task to memorize my message for mine is much longer than Washington's message."

I said, "It may take me a little longer, but I think I can memorize it." The General had finished his message which nearly filled a page. He handed it to me and said that he and Mrs. Thomas had an appointment in the city. This would give me some time to memorize the new message. They bade me "Goodbye" till they should come back.

They were away for an hour and a half, and when they returned, I handed the General his written message. Then, I repeated the message to him by memory.
"That is admirable. You have it verbatim, my dear young lady," said the General.
"Let us talk a bit more in the parlor," and he led the way.

In the parlor, I noticed there was a piano. Mrs. Thomas noticed that I was excited to see the piano and asked if I played. When I said "yes", she asked if I could play for them. So, I sat down and played some popular patriotic pieces that were all the rage at that time. General and Mrs. Thomas were delighted and applauded.

Then, the General stepped to one of the front windows and looked through the partly-closed shutters. He turned and exclaimed "Miss Wilson, we shall soon have all New York in front of our house if you continue playing. Just look out in the street and see the crowd. However, I can see some British officers (by their redcoats) who may not relish the patriotic pieces you have been playing."

"Well," I said, "I will play something more agreeable to their taste" and I struck up "God Save the King," "Britannia Rules The Waves" and other British favorites. Then, after a few psalm tunes, I closed with "Old One Hundred".

After lingering for a few minutes, and hearing no more music, the crowd gave three cheers and dispersed very quietly. This was a great relief to General and Mrs. Thomas. They were fearful that some of the pieces I had played might anger the British officers and lead to trouble. We then retired again to the sitting room and, after partaking of some cake and wine, I went to bed for some well-deserved sleep.

The next morning after breakfast, I said goodbye to my kind hostess, who very affectionately invited me to visit them whenever I visited the city.

I left them with my market basket on my arm, purchased a little sugar, tea and some other small matters and hastened homeward. I found no difficulty in passing the sentinels and, towards evening, reached home. My family was relieved to see me unharmed and asked me all about my adventure.

The next day, I went to General Washington's headquarters. After greeting me, he offered me congratulations on the success of my mission.

Then, I repeated the return message from General Thomas while he wrote it down. He said that he had no doubt that the message was correct. As I was about to leave, he said, " You must not go without dinner."

It would have been impolite to refuse, so I had dinner with General Washington and two other American officers.

After dinner, the General offered me several gold pieces for my valuable services (as he called them) but I refused to accept them and said, "If my mission proves to be of any service to my country, I shall consider myself amply repaid. But if you will give me one of those small pistoles on the counter as a souvenir, then I may have the pride of saying, many years from now, "This was given to me by General Washington". I will take the smallest."

"I would be happy to do that," he said. "I just regret that I do not have a more valuable keepsake to give to you." He handed me a Spanish pistole, worth about $ 3.60. Even today, I would not sell it for all of the money in the world.

"And so, children, that is the story of my adventure as a spy for General George Washington. The wind and snow have calmed down and the fire is burning down, so I think this is a good time to go to bed. "

"Sleep well, children."

Stephen Wilson (1802 - 1891) says the following in his journal:

"Some years later, my aunt, Elizabeth Wilson (1757 - 1855) married a man by the name of Fowler but they had no children. After his death, she married Enoch Homes, and they lived for some years in the upper part of what was then Luzerne, now called Lackawanna County, PA, at a place called Capouse; not far from Scranton. They moved from there to the western part of New York State; then, from there to Canada, where Aunt Elizabeth died at the age of ninety-eight."

"Elizabeth and Enoch had 3 children. Their only son, Benjamin, remained in New York state. He married a Miss Alsworth in 1811, and, with his bride, visited us. We then lived in the old Ferry House on the west side of the Susquehanna, right opposite your Uncle Taylor's mansion. I recollect Cousin Ben from his introduction of his young wife to father as well as if occured yesterday. It was "Uncle, this is my girl!" and she was a very pretty young woman. Benjamin had two sisters, Amy and Eunice; I cannot say much of them. The last time I ever saw Uncle Homes' family together was in the winter of 1808, when they lived at Capouse.
I also visited Benjamin in 1822 in Lockport, NY."

Author

This is Charles Courtsal's first book.
He has no qualifications as an artist, writer or publisher, but has sent and received secret messages for decades as a Professor of Primary Care Medicine at the University of Rochester School of Medicine.

He and his crafty wife, Lisa, are the proud parents of one son, Brendan, who is not very good at keeping secrets.

They live in a house full of projects in Rochester, NY.

Illustrator

Kitty has carefully balanced her intelligence and prudence as an oncology nurse for 39 years. In addition, she has always had a passion for the creative arts.

She was a kindergarten teacher for 6 years (bulletin boards were her medium). She was also a daring and spirited modern dancer for 15 years.

She has always loved to draw, so she was thrilled when her dear friend Charlie asked her to illustrate his book.

Kitty also lives in Rochester, NY.

Here are some questions for you along with some more information about this story

The spy in this true story was Elizabeth Wilson. Her nephew, Stephen Wilson, was one
of the children present during the snowstorm at the beginning of the book. He wrote down her story in his journal as a
letter to his niece, Clara, in 1887. You can see the actual journal by clicking here: chasefamilyletters.blogspot.com (October
2015 post).

Did you know that the marbled paper on the cover of this book and the writing on the inside covers of this book are taken
from the actual journal?
I bet some of your family members tell you interesting stories about your family as well. Who could you talk with to learn
about these stories in your family? How can you record those stories for the children of your children?

How did I obtain Stephen Wilson's journal?

In 1956, a new tenant was moving into a house on Academy Street in Wilkes-Barre, Pennsylvania. As the tenant explored
the attic, they found a small packet of papers that had belonged to the previous occupant of the house, Thomas Taylor. The
tenant knew that Frances Brooks Chase was Thomas Taylor's niece, so they contacted her and gave her the packet of papers. This journal was in that packet. As Frances was getting older, she knew that her great niece, Frances Chase Courtsal,
was interested in their family history, so she gave the journal to her. Frances C. Courtsal was my mother, so when she died
in 2008, the journal came to me. As a reminder, you can see Our Family Tree on page 4.

As a child, my mother told me the story of "Elizabeth the Spy" many times, but I had never seen the story written down.
Can you imagine how surprised I was to find Elizabeth's story in the journal that came to me? The story was so special to
me that I decided I would share it with you in this book.

Are there any old books or belongings in your house that you could ask your family about? Where did they come from?
Who used these tools? Who read these books?

Tale of Spying in Revolutionary Days Found in Wilkes - Barre Attic

This was the headline of the article in the Wilkes-Barre Record newspaper when Stephen Wilson's journal was discovered
in June of 1956. You can see the newspaper and read the article by clicking here: chasefamilyletters.blogspot.com (June
2021 post).

Amelia Press
NFB Publishing
Buffalo, New York
NFBPublishing.com

...of York State, fr...
...anada, when Aunt 6...
...t the age of ninety-ei...
...ly son Benjamin re...
...ate. I visited him...
...ockport. He married...
...lsworth, and with his...
...e then lived at the...
...the west side of the,
...ght opposite your Un...
...ansion. I recollect
...my his introduction.
...ife to father as well
...ster day. It was, "U...

daughters — Uriah Jr
beth, Elnathan and th
in the Revolutinary
as captain and Ja
day your grandfathe
also entered the army
lay at White Plai
above New York. Elb
sian, acted as a spy
I have writen quite a a
transaction as relate
they,sixty years ago. E
ds married a man b
Fowler, and after his

CPSIA information can be obtained
at www.ICGtesting.com
Printed in the USA
LVHW072014051221
705330LV00002B/76